The World's Stupidest

Celebrities

D1428513

The World's Stupidest

Celebrities

LUCIE CAVE

Michael O'Mara Humour

First published in Great Britain in 2005 by
Michael O'Mara Books Limited
9 Lion Yard, Tremadoc Road
London SW4 7NQ

A CIP catalogue record for this book is available from the
British Library

ISBN 1-84317-137-6

1 3 5 7 9 10 8 6 4 2

www.mombooks.com

Designed and typeset by K DESIGN, Winscombe, Somerset

Printed and bound in Great Britain
by Cox & Wyman Ltd, Reading, Berks

Introduction

They have special wardrobes for their knickers, jacuzzis in their offices (when they *do* work, that is) and ferrets as pets. Celebrities live in a world where it's customary to bathe in champagne one moment and then bitch about the rigours of fame the next. But who's complaining? It's these foibles, quirks and strange obsessions that make the rich and famous the fascinating species they are, and that sell millions of pounds' worth of tabloid newspapers, magazines, films and records.

Blissfully unaware of their eccentricities, stars roam the globe unchecked and oblivious to the fact that their egos have inflated to Jordan's boobesque proportions. From the captains of the don't-you-know-who-I-am? syndrome, and masters of not-thinking-before-they-speak – this book highlights a whole dressing-room full of celebrity comedies of errors. We also pay homage to some of the sillier mistakes they've made while believing they're invisible to the law (and to their partners, for that matter).

So when you put your foot in it at work or say something you wish you hadn't, the chances are some stupid star has done it first (and much, much worse); just be grateful that you won't read about it in the newspaper the next day . . .

Sucky Sucky Long Time

Notorious lady-lover Calum Best unwittingly showed the world his moves when he was caught getting down and dirty with model and daughter of Mick Jagger, Lizzie Jagger. The amorous pair had ordered a taxi to take them somewhere more 'private' after a party in London, but the frisky couple just couldn't wait for their carriage and started, ahem, getting better acquainted on the stairs. Problem was, these stairs were under the direct view of the club's CCTV camera and the pictures were printed in all their glory in a Sunday newspaper the following week.

✦ ✦ ✦

*'I was thinking about dying the other day
. . . the death thought came while I was sitting on
the toilet peeing – that's where I have my most
contemplative thoughts.'*

MADONNA

✦ ✦ ✦

David's Disc

Tut tut. As Beckham and his pregnant wife Victoria
drove their son Brooklyn to The Film Works in
Manchester for a private screening of *Monsters Inc.* for
Brooklyn's birthday, photographers noticed the tax disc
had expired. In fact Brooklyn's party was beset by
motoring hiccups. Becks's Manchester United teammates
Mikael Silvestre and Laurent Blanc both parked illegally.
Blanc did not pay for a parking ticket and was clamped
and fined, while Silvestre left his car in a loading bay,
only to have parking attendants try to remove it. Luckily
for Silvestre, the vehicle was too heavy for the towing
equipment and he managed to rescue it just in time.

✦ ✦ ✦

*'Even if you have only two seconds, drop
everything and give him a blow job. That way, he
won't really want sex with anyone else.'*

JERRY HALL

> *'That would have won him the gold medal in the championship four years ago which he won anyway.'*

DES LYNAM

✦ ✦ ✦

Mandarin Martin

Singer Ricky Martin might be more orange than, well, an orange, but it seems that's not quite enough colour for the Latino singer. Whenever he appears in concert he insists on having a special orange light on stage to make him look 'glowing'.

✦ ✦ ✦

> *'I have to go . . . drop some kids in the pool.'*

JESSICA SIMPSON

Flat as a Pancake

Jamie Oliver, the scooter-riding, cheeky-chappie celebrity chef was asked to appear on *The Oprah Winfrey Show* in 2003, and its producers thought it would be a great stunt for Oliver to enter stage left on his scooter, to which the Naked Chef readily agreed. 'The thing was, the floor was really polished and the tyres brand new,' he recalled. 'Before I knew it, I stacked it, flew about a metre in the air, and landed on my chest. I had a really silky body warmer on and I slid about three metres with my arms in some sort of Superman pose, using my chin as a brake.' Rumours that Jamie is about to venture into Meals on Wheels are unconfirmed . . .

✦ ✦ ✦

'Moving from Wales to Italy is like moving to a different country.'

IAN RUSH

Car Wars

He might be nifty with a light sabre but actor Ewan McGregor isn't such a dab hand with everyday equipment. During filming for the movie *Big Fish*, one scene required him to drive and park a cherry-red Dodge car. One onlooker recalled, 'He couldn't parallel park to save his life. He's supposed to be driving the getaway car and Steve Buscemi is the trigger man, but they had to wait for Mr McGregor to park the car. Poor guy, it took him seven tries to finally get it right.'

✦ ✦ ✦

'I expect to win it. Sit back, put your feet up in front of the TV, relax and enjoy it. Let me do the worrying – that's what I get paid for.'

England manager GRAHAM TAYLOR before the 1992 European Championships. England didn't win a game

'I want a world without war, a world without insanity. I want to see people do well. I don't even think it's as much as what I want for myself. It's more what I want for the people around me. That's what I want.'

TOM CRUISE

✦ ✦ ✦

I Haven't Got a Big Head

After his near-fatal car accident in January 2004, singer Daniel Bedingfield decided to throw an 'I'm not dead' party for his family and friends. As a special treat for the lucky guests he left the car he'd crashed on the drive outside – complete with blood on the windscreen. Why? 'So people could see they almost lost me and realize how good it was that I'm still here,' he said.

> *'Our enemies are innovative and resourceful, and so are we. They never stop thinking about new ways to harm our country and our people, and neither do we.'*

GEORGE W. BUSH

✦ ✦ ✦

Watch Out

Musicians Usher and Kanye West are such big fans of themselves that they own personalized watches . . . with their faces on. Following the MTV Video Music Awards in August 2005, West's pal Damon Dash gave him an 18-carat-gold, 7.5-carat-diamond watch with his face on. When jealous old Usher caught a glimpse of the flashy accessory, he ordered himself a 9.5-carat version – at a cost of $85,000.

✦ ✦ ✦

> *'I was asked to come to Chicago because Chicago is one of our fifty-two states.'*

RAQUEL WELCH on *Larry King Live*; there are only fifty States

Dream on, David

In May 2004, a modest David Hasselhoff claimed he had been partly responsible for the collapse of the Berlin Wall. Back in November 1989, on the night it was destroyed, the actor-turned-singer had performed 'Looking for Freedom' on the wall for his German fans. This, apparently, is what he considered to be so intrinsic to its downfall. He told a curator at the museum, 'I find it a bit sad that there is no photo of me hanging on the walls in the Berlin museum.'

✦ ✦ ✦

'I love kids. I was a kid myself, once.'

TOM CRUISE

✦ ✦ ✦

Beach Feet

At the beach, writer F. Scott Fitzgerald would bury his feet in the sand so strangers couldn't look at them.

Rourke Walks

After the producers of the film *Luck of the Draw* refused to cast his pet chihuahua in the movie, Mickey Rourke walked off the set. Rourke later went on to explain why he loves chihuahuas so much. He said, 'I live alone, and little dogs live twice as long as the bigger ones. So, if they're my family, I want them around as long as possible. When I come home and there's seven fuckin' cheerful things waiting, it's like coming home to a happy family that you just can't wait to see every day.' A priest was even called in to offer support after the death of pooch Beau Jack. Rourke said, 'I gave him mouth-to-mouth for forty-five minutes before they peeled me off. Depressed? He died at my home, and I didn't go back for two weeks.'

✦ ✦ ✦

'For NASA, space is still a high priority.'

DAN QUAYLE

'If I was just normally intelligent, I could probably get away with it – but I'm fiercely intelligent and that's threatening.'

SHARON STONE

+ + +

Two for Blue

Boy-band Blue's Lee Ryan lost his driving licence in 2003 for cutting up a police car while twice over the legal drink-drive limit. Pulling up alongside the constabulary at traffic lights, he suddenly swung his Porsche 911 Carrera in front of them when the lights changed. His excuse? 'Sorry, my bird rang me on the phone.'

It later emerged that the 'bird' in question was one of two that Mr Ryan had to occupy him that night. He confided to police officers that he'd just left the house of one lady friend and was in a rush to see another. Funnily enough, that didn't help his case.

Choice words

Daniel Bedingfield ended his six-week romance with PR girl Sam Almon in 2005 claiming he was looking for a girlfriend who could become a muse for his music. The singer claimed that he couldn't possibly pursue a serious relationship with her because she didn't inspire him enough. 'I'm single. Sam is beautiful, she's lovely, but she's not my girlfriend. When I have a girlfriend she'll be the theme for many albums. She needs to be so interesting and complex – and yet simple – that you can just continually use her as a muse.'

✦ ✦ ✦

'I never watched anybody make love, so how do you know if you're doing it right?'

KEVIN COSTNER

It's All About Mariah

Mariah Carey welcomed in her thirty-fifth year with a life-sized sponge and praline-butter-cream creation of herself – not a conventional birthday cake, it must be said. Standing six-foot tall, it was crafted by over a dozen chefs from London store Harrods, and cost approximately £5,000.

✦ ✦ ✦

'I thought chickens ate cheese.'

Big Brother 3's JADE GOODY

✦ ✦ ✦

Whisper Whisper

Movie star Joan Crawford hired an assistant to be present on the set of her pictures and whisper compliments into her ear between takes.

'I performed at Mom and Dad's party when I was four. Oh my gosh, I was singing a Madonna song and I peed myself.'

BRITNEY SPEARS

✦ ✦ ✦

She's Not Kidding

At the premiere of the film *The Interpreter* in London in 2005, society girl Tamara Beckwith got a small round of sarcastic applause as, rather late into the proceedings, she found her seat. Rather than realizing people were taking the mickey, Ms Beckwith whispered to her companion, 'How funny, they must have thought I was Nicole Kidman.'

✦ ✦ ✦

'I can't really remember the names of the clubs that we went to.'

SHAQUILLE O'NEILL, on whether he had visited the Parthenon during his visit to Greece

'Music, sex and family are my greatest pleasures.
Sex and family are the same thing to me.'

SIMON LE BON

✦ ✦ ✦

Gay's the Way

Singer Mariah Carey once stated that the only time she flirts with a man is when she suspects he's gay; nevertheless, she loves flirting. She said, 'I'm a big flirt – even though the fame thing hinders my flirtability. Even if I'm flirting mildly, the guy takes it as, "Oh, she likes me!" Then, because I don't go home with every Tom, Dick and Harry, I'll spend the entire night steering him away from that idea. So I can only do it with guys I think might be gay.'

'For the first time in my life I cried incredible gurgling tears of happiness and it was the most cleansing feeling and the most wonderful feeling that I've ever had.'

JENNIFER LOPEZ on the moment Ben Affleck proposed

✦ ✦ ✦

Pinching Paris

As if she hadn't seen herself enough times already, Paris Hilton decided to steal a copy of her own DVD, *One Night In Paris*, from a newsstand, shouting the words, 'I'm taking this and I'm not buying it!' The multi-millionaire was then faced with charges of theft and vandalism, although ultimately the District Attorney didn't prosecute.

✦ ✦ ✦

'It's the sort of vague calm you get after vomiting where the vomit itself is rather unpleasant but when it's over it does bring you a kind of strange peace and that's how I feel.'

BEN AFFLECK after his break up with Jennifer Lopez

Harrison's Heaven

When Harrison Ford was asked by a reporter, 'If Heaven exists, what would you want God to say to you at the pearly gates?' Ford replied, 'You're a lot better looking in person.'

✦ ✦ ✦

'I love being in America.'

CHARLOTTE CHURCH on stage in Toronto

✦ ✦ ✦

Loo-pez

It seems despite coming *from* one, Jenny from the block doesn't like being caught *in* a block – of toilets, that is; fans wanting her autograph always hang around outside. She says, 'People follow you into the bathroom. They listen to you pee, wait for you to come out of the stall, and then ask to shake your hand or sign the loo roll.'

'Whenever I watch TV and see those poor starving kids all over the world, I can't help but cry. I mean I'd love to be skinny like that, but not with all those flies and death and stuff.'

MARIAH CAREY

✦ ✦ ✦

Cash For No Questions

Comic actor John Belushi liked to borrow twenty-dollar bills from all of his  new acquaintances so he could judge what they'd be like as friends by how they reacted to his request.

✦ ✦ ✦

'I can do anything you want me to do as long as I don't have to speak.'

LINDA EVANGELISTA

Food For Thought

Paris Hilton is so pampered that she expects other people to read the menu to her when she's in a restaurant. The blonde socialite  was eating out with her *Baywatch* mate Pamela Anderson when she lost the plot because no one would read its contents to her. Pam told a magazine interviewer, 'She slammed the menu down and screamed, "I hate reading! Someone tell me what's on the menu!" I mean, I'm blonde but c'mon.'

✦ ✦ ✦

'I know that if you leave dishes in the sink they get sticky and hard to wash the next day.'

ARNOLD SCHWARZENEGGER

✦ ✦ ✦

'Platypus? I thought it was pronounced "platymapus". Has it always been pronounced platypus?'

JESSICA SIMPSON

'Beyond its entertainment value, Baywatch *has enriched and, in many cases, helped save lives. I'm looking forward to the opportunity to continue with a project which has had such significance for so many.'*

DAVID HASSELHOFF

✦ ✦ ✦

Fish Fancies

Diva Mariah Carey once told reporters she practised 'extra caution' when petting dolphins during her trips around the world – for fear of turning the sea creatures on.

✦ ✦ ✦

'I've always been a bit maturer than what I am.'

SAMANTHA FOX

Lucky Escape

Leonardo DiCaprio asked staff at the World Cafe, Santa Monica, to 'immediately remove' a customer who had asked him to autograph his arse. The signature seeker was then promptly ushered out of the door. He didn't mind though. He hadn't paid his bill!

✦ ✦ ✦

Waller's World

Pop Idol reject, twenty-stone Rik Waller, launched a twenty-six date tour in 2004, convinced that 'people are more impressed by voice than looks.' When he only managed to sell two tickets to his Devon gig, Rick was forced to cancel the rest of the tour.

Pay Up!

While treating then girlfriend Kate Bosworth to a gourmet meal at Casaro Amarelo in Rio de Janeiro, Brazil, in January 2005, Hollywood star Orlando Bloom found himself unable to pay a $760 restaurant bill, and then, after promising to cough up, didn't. To his embarrassment, his credit card was declined due to a technical hitch. The restaurant's owner admits she's still waiting to hear from the *Lord of the Rings* actor. She says, 'He told us he didn't have a personal email account and so took our address. And although we're sure it's a complete misunderstanding and know he's very busy, we've yet to hear from him.'

✦ ✦ ✦

'Well, I think if you say you're going to do something and don't do it, that's trustworthiness.'

GEORGE W. BUSH

Wayne's women

Naughty, naughty. Soon after being crowned football's new golden boy, it emerged that Wayne Rooney had slept with prostitutes behind fiancée Colleen McLoughlin's back. Not only was one a 48-year-old grandma with the oh-so-flattering nickname 'Auld Slapper', but on one occasion, rather than trying to hide his identity, he spent his visit signing autographs in the waiting room. One of his notes read: 'To Charlotte, I shagged you on 28 Dec., Wayne Rooney.'

✦ ✦ ✦

'Crucifixes are sexy because they've got a naked man on the front.'

MADONNA

'Who pissed?!! Who pissed on my fucking carpet!?! That bastard fucking dog man. I'm going to throw you in the pool! It's a fucking terrorist man! It's fucking part of Bin Laden's gang!'

OZZY OSBOURNE

✦ ✦ ✦

Leaky Lineker

A European Championship match against Ireland in 1988 found England's Gary Lineker with a rather upset stomach. Shortly after kick-off, the inevitable had happened and the term 'follow through' applied to more than his passing. Ever resourceful, Lineker made a sliding tackle, depriving a midfielder of the ball and disposing of the problem in his shorts at the same time.

Top of the class

When a US fan sent David Beckham a hooded top as a present, he liked it so much he wore it for his twenty-sixth-birthday photocall. He was later shocked to hear that the picture on the front was of Nazi Adolf Eichmann. Beckham, whose grandfather is Jewish, said he'd never wear the top again.

✦ ✦ ✦

'My best friend is a rock. They're very inspirational . . . every colour, every texture [in my menswear collection] has been inspired by sitting on this rock. It's wonderful for menswear, but I find rocks very female.'

DONNA KARAN

Steamy Windows

When former England footballer Stan Collymore admitted trawling car parks for casual sex, a new word barked its way into the English dictionary. 'Dogging' was described by Collymore as a sexual activity 'in which strangers meet to observe or take part in sexual encounters'. Following his revelation, BBC Radio Five Live said it would no longer use Collymore as a commentator. Why not? He clearly knows how to score.

✦ ✦ ✦

'I'm just totally normal. And that's why I'm in trouble, because I'm normal and slightly arrogant . . . A lot of people don't like themselves and I happen to be totally in love with myself.'

MIKE TYSON

'Rod [Stewart] came into my life six weeks after
I parted from Lou [Adler] and I rose back into the
sky like a gull whose oil-soaked wings had been
cleansed with detergent.'

BRITT EKLAND

✦ ✦ ✦

All White

Zoe Lucker, the star of the hit British television series
Footballers' Wives, filmed a scene where her character,
tarty Tanya Turner, snorted cocaine. She recalls,
travelling home on the train, 'These two guys eyed me up
. . . I rubbed my nose and white rocks [of fake cocaine]
fell out on to my black top. They just looked at me as if
I had a real problem!'

✦ ✦ ✦

'Twenty-three is old. It's almost twenty-five, which
is, like, almost mid-twenties.'

JESSICA SIMPSON

'I hate dead people.'

PARIS HILTON

✦ ✦ ✦

G8 . . . or Summit Like That

In October 2004, Gazza announced he was changing his name to 'G8', in an attempt to be taken more seriously. G8, he said, was a combination of the first initial of his surname (Gascoigne) and the number of his old football shirt. Rather than achieving the required result, however, one of the first headlines to be written about him *après* the name change was, 'Who G8 all the pies?'

✦ ✦ ✦

'If he were here I'd ask if I could lick his eyeballs.'

CHRISTIAN SLATER on Jack Nicholson

It Wasn't Me!

Fiery actor Sean Penn served thirty-two days in jail in 1987 for assaulting an extra who had taken his photograph on the set of *Colors*. Ten years later, Penn was approached by another photographer, and, after a scuffle, the photographer accused Penn of hitting him with a rock. Penn's version differed somewhat; the actor claimed he'd merely picked up a rock to defend himself, and that the photographer had sustained his injury as a result of having lunged at the rock while Penn was holding it.

✦ ✦ ✦

Tucker's Luck

Rush Hour star Chris Tucker pleaded guilty to speeding and eluding police during a brief car chase in April 2005. Tucker was driving a Bentley at 109 mph on a stretch of road with a 70-mph speed limit when Georgia state troopers attempted to pull him over. The comedian told authorities that he didn't hear their sirens because . . . he was on his way to church.

Not-so-clever Carey

When singer Mariah Carey was told of the death of the King Hussein of Jordan in 1999 she relayed to CNN her devastation. 'I'm inconsolable at the present time. I was a very good friend of Jordan. He was probably the greatest basketball player this country has ever seen. We will never see his like again.' When told that it was King Hussein of Jordan who had died, rather than Michael Jordan, Carey was led away by her security men in a state of 'confusion'.

✦ ✦ ✦

REPORTER: *Did you read the original Shakespearean version of* Othello?

ACTOR LAURENCE FISHBURNE *(starring in* Othello *in which two-thirds of the dialogue was cut)*: *Why should I read all those words that I'm not going to get to say?*

Apocalypse Now? Nah . . .

After production had begun in the
Philippines on *Apocalypse Now*, a
crew member warned director
Francis Ford Coppola that
seasonal typhoons were a threat
to his sets. 'What are you,'
Coppola replied, 'a fucking
weatherman?' A few weeks later, the budding
weatherman was proved hilariously (and expensively)
right, when a tropical storm destroyed most of
Coppola's set.

✦ ✦ ✦

*'It felt wonderful doing it. But that's rather like
urinating in brown velvet pants. It can feel
wonderful, but no one will watch.'*

ROBIN WILLIAMS on starring in *Dead Poets Society*

'What would happen if you melted? You know, you never really hear this talked about that much, but spontaneous combustion? It exists! People burn from within . . . sometimes they'll be in a wooden chair and the chair won't burn, but there'll be nothing left of the person. Except sometimes the teeth. Or the heart. No one speaks about this – but it's for real.'

KEANU REEVES

✦ ✦ ✦

Ickle Iglesias . . .

Confusing a magazine interview with a confessional, lovely Latino Enrique Iglesias perhaps let his mouth run away with him. 'If you had the biggest penis in the world, you would sell records. But I don't. I could actually have the smallest penis in the world out there.'

Galling

During one of his shows on Virgin Radio, ginger host Chris Evans told listeners that prior to flying to Greece with Billie Piper, he'd parked his £60,000 Jaguar XK8 at Charles de Gaulle airport and that the keys were on the top of the offside rear wheel. A listener went to the airport hoping to drive it back to England only to find someone else had already taken it.

✦ ✦ ✦

Drinking Diva

Being the loving wife she is, Sharon Osbourne used on occasion to confiscate rocker Ozzy's clothes to stop him from stealing from his house to frequent bars. Not to be daunted, Ozzy took to wearing Sharon's clothes instead. 'I ended up in some pretty weird places. I remember being in Frankfurt, Germany, one time and I've got this green evening dress on, or blue or whatever. And the guy behind the bar goes, "You do not belong in this bar. You must go down to the bar down the road!" It was one of them transvestite bars.'

Universally Challenged

Jeremy Paxman shocked a university audience by announcing that news presenting was a job for 'trained chimpanzees' (before adding that his own job, as anchorman for BBC2's *Newsnight*, was the exception). He made the comment during a debate about the role of presenters, politicians and the media at Cambridge University. ITV later said, 'We've always known the BBC was a bit of a zoo.'

✦ ✦ ✦

'I need someone I have verbal and spiritual collateral with, where I can go to the bank and withdraw some of her feelings and knowledge.'

SYLVESTER STALLONE

> *'Colin Farrell used to live above me. He was the guy on the sixth floor who kept calling the fucking police. It's funny that he's the wild party guy now.'*
>
> JA RULE

✦ ✦ ✦

Win D'oh

In his 2004 biography *Feel*, Robbie Williams recounted a story from the days when he wasn't quite as clean living as he is now. During a party at U2 singer Bono's Dublin retreat, where some 'exotic' mushrooms were on the menu, Bono later found Williams staring at what he thought was a picture, claiming it was the most beautiful work of art he'd ever seen. 'Robbie,' pointed out Bono, 'that's the window.'

'I get ten bags of M&Ms and tip them on a table. Then I sort them out into little piles of all the same colours. You know all the reds together, all the yellows.'

USHER

✦ ✦ ✦

Motormouth Madge

During Madonna's first appearance on *The Late Show with David Letterman*, the singer's remarks had to be bleeped out more than a dozen times, and her next appearance was not much more distinguished – she admitted to peeing on her feet in the shower because it killed off fungal organisms.

✦ ✦ ✦

'Good-looking people turn me off. Myself included.'

PATRICK SWAYZE

'I may believe in Santa, but I'm not delusional.'

✦ ✦ ✦

Señorita Slip-up

In 2001, Geri Halliwell stunned Spanish television viewers when the presenter of the show *El Informal* asked her, in Spanish, to perform some yoga skills. Geri, (who is half Spanish), tried to reply 'Will you do yoga with me?' but what she actually said was 'Will you do yoga on my fanny?' While the Spanish audience sat dumbfounded, Geri went on to perform her yoga moves, completely oblivious to her slip-up.

✦ ✦ ✦

'Sometimes we have to try on wool before we get cashmere. But it's really important to experience polyester.'

GERI HALLIWELL on men

'So, where's the Cannes Film Festival being held this year?'

CHRISTINA AGUILERA

✦ ✦ ✦

'We've got to pause and ask ourselves: how much clean air do we need?'

LEE IACOCCA, Chairman of the Chrysler corporation

✦ ✦ ✦

'In an action film you act in the action, in a drama film you act in the drama.'

JEAN-CLAUDE VAN DAMME

✦ ✦ ✦

'Not only was Sue having a nervous breakdown, but she was having a really tough time mentally, too.'

SIMON BATES

'The world is more like it is now than it ever
has before.'

DWIGHT D. EISENHOWER

✦ ✦ ✦

'China is a big country, inhabited by
many Chinese.'

CHARLES DE GAULLE

✦ ✦ ✦

'A proof is a proof. What kind of proof? It's a
proof. A proof is proof. And when you have a good
proof, it's because it is proven.'

JEAN CHRÉTIEN

✦ ✦ ✦

'I was recently on a tour of Latin America, and the
only regret I have was that I didn't study Latin
harder in school so I could converse with
these people.'

DAN QUAYLE

Britney's Boob

While promoting her album, Britney was asked by a Spanish journalist if she liked Spain's music. 'Yes, I really like it,' she said. 'From Paulina Rubio to Kylie Minogue.' When the interviewer pointed out that Kylie was Australian and Paulina Mexican, she sheepishly replied, 'I still think they're great.'

✦ ✦ ✦

Dirty Diana

During the time he was working on his aptly named solo album, *Off The Wall*, Michael Jackson decided to stop washing and changing his clothes. Like Jackson's personal hygiene, the situation deteriorated until his producer, Quincy Jones, began to call Jackson 'Smelly'. When Jackson found out, Jones attempted to extricate himself from the situation by telling Mikey that 'smelly' was a slang term meaning 'cool'.

*'Why do people treat me with fun just because I
am the biggest, strongest and most beautiful man
in the world?'*

ARNOLD SCHWARZENEGGER

✦ ✦ ✦

Food for Thought

In the late seventies, Michael Jackson held an interview
at a posh French eatery in New York. The story goes that
Michael popped a napkin in his T-shirt and began to eat
his Caesar salad . . . with his hands. Then, when a slice of
quiche arrived, he poked it with his finger, before picking
it up and shoving it in his mouth, declaring, 'It's just like
ham and eggs!'

✦ ✦ ✦

*'I sound vain, but I could probably make a
difference for almost everyone I ever met if I chose
to involve myself with them either professionally or
personally.'*

KEVIN COSTNER

'Smoking kills. If you're killed, you've lost a very important part of your life.'

✦ ✦ ✦

Dirty Words

Unfortunately, while visiting America in 1995 to promote Jean-Paul Rappeneau's *The Horseman on the Roof* in which he was starring, Kylie's current squeeze, the actor Olivier Martinez, suffered something of a verbal misunderstanding. 'I spent two weeks,' Martinez recalled, 'telling people "I love to ride whores."'

✦ ✦ ✦

'We're going to turn this team around 360 degrees.'

Tat-who?

The peril of having tattoos dedicated to loved ones came home to rocker Tommy Lee after Pamela Anderson made him alter his 'Heather' tattoo (inspired by Heather Locklear) to 'eather'. To show her own devotion, she also went under the needle and imaginatively came up with 'Tommy'. Following the couple's split some time later, Anderson had the tattoo altered so that it read 'Mommy'.

✦ ✦ ✦

'If I saw an alien, I'd tell it to fuck right off because whatever planet he came from they wouldn't have The Beatles or any decent fucking music.'

LIAM GALLAGHER

A White Old Mistake

During a visit to the White House, *The Dukes of Hazzard* actress Jessica Simpson met the Secretary of the Interior, Gale A. Norton. 'You've done a nice job,' Jessica told her, 'decorating the White House . . . ' Jess later explained her cryptic remark: 'I thought that she was the Secretary of Interior *Design*!'

✦ ✦ ✦

Tat-too Late

Having been converted to the beliefs of Jewish mysticism by her mate Madonna, Britney Spears decided to get a Kabbalah-inspired tattoo on her neck (despite the fact that the Jewish faith forbids tattoos). So off she went to the tattoo parlour and bagged herself an ink inscription that she hoped meant 'mysterious'. Unfortunately, it actually meant 'strange'.

'I was in history class and the teacher said to raise your hand if you know the continents. I raised my hand and said, "A, E, I, O, U!" And the teacher replied, "Those aren't even consonants . . . they're vowels!"'

JESSICA SIMPSON

✦ ✦ ✦

Oops, She Did It Again!

In 2004, Britney Spears also had some Japanese symbols tattooed on her hipbone. 'Britney was absolutely devastated,' her friend (and actress) Taryn Manning later reported, 'when I told her that the symbols were complete gibberish.'

✦ ✦ ✦

'The second you stop learning stuff, man, you're dead.'

TOM CRUISE

> *'I'm so naive about finances. Once when my mother mentioned an amount and I didn't understand she had to explain: "That's like three Mercedes." Then I understood.'*

BROOKE SHIELDS

✦ ✦ ✦

Hindi Hiccup

David Beckham is also known for his penchant for tattoos, and regularly uses them as a way of expressing his affection for his family. Shame then, that the Hindi design he chose to spell out the name of wife Victoria was mistakenly drawn with the addition of one extra letter. His forearm now spells out 'Vihctoria'.

'I invented the Internet.'

AL GORE

✦ ✦ ✦

'She Loves You' (Not)

During a boozy evening with friends in a restaurant in Los Angeles, John Lennon popped into the ladies' bathroom, and, rather bizarrely, came back out with a sanitary towel stuck to his forehead. At the next club they visited Lennon, still wearing his bizarre headgear, made a real nuisance of himself, so much so that their waitress refused to wait on them. 'Don't you know who I am?' Lennon asked. 'Yeah,' the waitress replied. 'You're some asshole with a Kotex on his head!'

✦ ✦ ✦

'I hate cooking! I hate cleaning! Martha Stewart can lick my scrotum . . . Do I have a scrotum?'

SHARON OSBOURNE

Culkin Gets Caught

In 2004, former child star Macaulay Culkin (then aged twenty-four) was arrested for possession of illegal substances. Culkin was a passenger in a vehicle stopped for speeding, but during a routine search, officers discovered seventeen grams of marijuana, eight Xanax pills and sixteen round white pills identified as clonazepam, a sedative used to treat anxiety and seizures. Clever Culkin then told police he did not have a prescription for the pills.

◆ ◆ ◆

Hashed Off

US teenage pop star Aaron Carter was left blushing when the American tabloid the *National Enquirer* ran photos of him smoking the 'erb through a small bong. This came just one week after the singer insisted 'I don't do drugs' in a *People* magazine article. One of the clean-cut singer's 'pals' had come forward with the pictures that showed a topless Carter puffing marijuana fumes into the air during a daytime house party in 2003. Now that's what friends are for!

Bublé Head

Enjoying a celeb shindig at Leonardo DiCaprio's mansion, Canadian singer Michael Bublé ended up feeling slightly the worse for wear. 'Leo made a huge amount of tacos, which were delicious,' Bublé said, 'but I drank too much and started feeling sick. I went outside to get some fresh air but threw up in the pool. I was so embarrassed, I didn't dare to go back inside, so I climbed over his back wall and threw up in his bushes as I went. I'd left my wallet and keys in his house, so I had to walk miles home, and then sleep in my porch.'

✦ ✦ ✦

'During the delivery to speed things up, they grabbed these ice-picks [forceps] and yanked the baby out, paralysing his whole head and face and part of his body. His body was so deformed it was pathetic. The doctors told me, "He's so crippled you ought to put him away." But I decided he was going to walk, he was going to talk.'

JACKIE STALLONE, proud mother of Sylvester

Thanks, But No Thanks

Comedian Steve Coogan was left blushing when he sent a bottle of champagne over to Matthew Perry's table while both stars were dining at swish restaurant The Ivy. What Steve didn't realize was that the *Friends* star was a recovering alcoholic, and Perry promptly sent the champers back. Oops.

✦ ✦ ✦

'I let him do it and it felt so good. God, that pain is like nothing else in the world. And it's so sexual too, you know? I mean, after it's done you just want to go and drive a car off a cliff or something, you know?'

DREW BARRYMORE talking about having a tattoo

'I'm a highly, highly, highly creative human being.
I write music all the time. I write scripts constantly.
I run my own production company. I'm also a very
determined businesswoman. I've got a lot of things
to do and I don't have time to be classified as
difficult, and I don't have time to care.'

KIM BASINGER

✦ ✦ ✦

Pint of Puke

Northern comedian Johnny Vegas lived up to his
reputation as a drinking legend one evening in a London
pub. After requesting a pint glass at the bar, Johnny then
casually heaved into it an exact pint of vomit. With little
fuss, Vegas carried on drinking.

✦ ✦ ✦

'I have said that the sanction regime [against
Iraq] is like Swiss cheese. That meant that they
weren't very effective.'

GEORGE W. BUSH

Hamstar

In 2004, *Troy* actor Brad Pitt revealed a 'small' secret when he was asked whether he thought he represented the 'perfect male specimen'. Modestly, Brad replied, 'I don't know if that's true – I'm hung like a hamster.'

✦ ✦ ✦

Pitt's Penis

Brad Pitt and George Clooney were renowned for playing practical jokes on each other on the set of *Ocean's Twelve*. One particular incident left Mr Pitt red-faced after he drove around LA with a sign on his car stating 'Small Penis Onboard', which had been put there by none other than George Clooney. That's what you get for saying you're hung like a hamster.

'Smoke can drive me mad. Otherwise, it's not getting things you've paid for. That's why we used to smash up hotels – not because we had nothing better to do, but because you're paying top money and you weren't getting any respect.'

ROD STEWART

✦ ✦ ✦

A Tale of Two Tramps

During the filming of *Ocean's Twelve* in Italy, stars Brad Pitt and George Clooney were shocked when the skies opened up and torrential rain followed. Their plan to take shelter in a posh Italian hotel sadly backfired, however, when the hotel doorman mistook the actors for vagrants and refused to let them in.

'I build my body to carry my brain around.'

SYLVESTER STALLONE

✦ ✦ ✦

Clooney the Clown

Is it true that when George Clooney's attended parties he's been known to borrow other people's cameras when they're not looking, take a picture of his own derrière, and then return the camera? Some sources say so . . .

✦ ✦ ✦

'Whenever I turn on TV I am reminded of the millions of women who have stringy hair, large pores, overweight figures and rough hands.'

WARREN BEATTY

Lullaby Lopez

Jennifer Lopez has a bizarre way of sending herself to sleep – by falling asleep to cookery shows. Her reason? So there won't be any rude awakenings if she dozes off. She explains, 'I know that if I fall asleep to it that no gunshots are gonna come on or anything like that. Sometimes, when you leave the TV on and news at night and everything, you know, weird stuff comes on and you wake from your sleep and you say, "What's going on?" There's never going to be any noise with cake and stuff on the food channel.' No, apart from a loud ping from the microwave!

✦ ✦ ✦

'The Beatles? They're on the wane.'

THE DUKE OF EDINBURGH in 1965

Bride Britney

Given that 2004 hosted two Britney weddings, it was
pretty clear what her New Year's resolution was that
year. At 4.30 a.m. on 3 January, Brit donned her best
ripped jeans and wed a lumberjack shirt from her
hometown named Jason Alexander. It lasted, ooooh,
all of fifty-five hours.

✦ ✦ ✦

Shoe Share

Comedian and actor Will Ferrell rotates his shoe usage
because he has such a large collection. He says, 'I like to
organize my shoes. I have a rotation cycle, so each shoe
gets worn the same amount. No shoe is left behind. Equal
opportunity.'

'Just remember folks, next Monday night Password
will be seen on Thursday evening.'

US *Password* game-show host ALLEN LUDDEN

✦ ✦ ✦

Tree Lee

Rocker Tommy Lee once took a horticulture course at
Nebraska University because of a love for trees. He said,
'There's this weird thing about me. I think I was a tree or
something in a past life. I've always been attracted to
nature, to trees.'

✦ ✦ ✦

'It was kind of boring for me to have to eat.
I would know that I had to, and I would.'

KATE MOSS

'I went in and said, "If I see one more gratuitous shot of a woman's body, I'm quitting . . ." I think the show should be emotional storylines, morals, real-life heroes. And that's what we're doing.'

DAVID HASSELHOFF, about *Baywatch*

+ + +

Hot Stuff

Franz Ferdinand frontman Alex Kapranos has an addiction to very spicy food that began while he was employed as a curry delivery driver in Glasgow, Scotland. 'I go through periods of compulsive addiction to chillies. I think you build up immunity to the heat. I'm at the stage where I need to stick three chillies on a slice of cheese on toast before I can taste them.' Steer clear, ladies . . .

+ + +

'You can hardly tell where the computer models finish and the real dinosaurs begin.'

LAURA DERN about the special effects
in the movie *Jurassic Park*

'The word "genius" isn't applicable in football.
A genius is a guy like Norman Einstein.'

JOE THEISMAN, quarterback and sports analyst

✦ ✦ ✦

Potty Pete

Hot on the heels of the infectious song 'Insania', complete with title taken from a word Peter Andre claimed to 'create' from 'insane' and 'mania', Mr Andre proved himself to be a true neologist by coming up with *another* new word. At a music event held in Kent in 2004, he was spotted whipping up a blend of filter coffee and green tea, which he then proclaimed to be 'Cofftea'. Crazy guy.

✦ ✦ ✦

'I owe a lot to my parents, especially my mother
and father.'

GREG NORMAN

'Sure there have been injuries and deaths in boxing – but none of them serious.'

ALAN MINTER, boxer

+ + +

Pretty Boy

Sir Paul McCartney wears ladies' false fingernails. The Beatles legend confessed he turned to the acrylic beauty aids to help him play the guitar. Macca agreed to try them after wife Heather suggested they would be the answer to his strumming woes.

+ + +

'Pitching is eighty per cent of the game. The other half is hitting and fielding.'

MICKEY RIVERS, baseball player

'I have a God-given talent. I got it from my dad.'

JULIAN WAKEFIELD, basketball player

+ + +

Funny Feet

Mariah Carey's love of stilettos comes with the
embarrassing consequence that she cannot
walk with her feet flat on the floor. The
singer has been a fan of heels ever
since she was a little child, and says:
'My feet repel flats – I have permanent high heels on.
Without knowing it, I walk on my tippy-toes with no
shoes on to the point that people laugh at me.'

+ + +

*'Saddam Hussein is a homicidal dictator who is
addicted to weapons of mass destruction.'*

GEORGE W. BUSH

Poo Did That?

Dogs may be a man's best friend but Ashton Kutcher, husband of Demi Moore, would probably not agree. The star, who started dating Moore in 2003, said, 'I have a weak stomach. One of Demi's dogs pooped in the living room the other day, and I didn't see it. The dog pooped, and I stepped in it. I started gagging and, like, throwing up. I could not handle it. Dog poop grosses me out.'

✦ ✦ ✦

'I think I'm more grounded, you know, and I know what I want out of life and I'm, you know, my morals are really, you know, strong and I have major beliefs about certain things and I think that has helped me, you know, from being, you know, coming from a really small town.'

BRITNEY SPEARS

Not So Smart(ie)

Duran Duran frontman Simon Le Bon's admission that he loved orange Smarties brought more trouble than he could have imagined. Fans responded enthusiastically, throwing them on stage during his concert performances. He soon realized, however, that 'Smarties aren't so great when they've been on a stage under hot spotlights. You tread on one and suddenly it releases this chocolate lubricant all over the stage that's more dangerous than a banana skin.' Maybe he would have preferred bon bons

✦ ✦ ✦

'I've always thought of the T-shirt as the Alpha and Omega of the fashion alphabet. The creative universe begins with its essentiality, and, whatever path the imagination takes, ends with its purity.'

GIORGIO ARMANI

Star Struck

When he was a youngster, *Apollo 13* star Kevin Bacon was amazed to discover that Dustin Hoffman – Rico 'Ratzo' Rizzo in *Midnight Cowboy* – was actually an actor. He admits, 'I was so blown away by this bum they got. I thought how did they get this bum to come and learn lines?' All became clear for Bacon when he saw Hoffman in the classic *The Graduate*.

✦ ✦ ✦

'The streets are safe in Philadelphia. It's only the people who make them unsafe.'

FRANK RIZZO, EX-POLICE CHIEF AND MAYOR OF PHILADELPHIA

Corr Blimey

During her time as a host of Channel 4's *The Big Breakfast*, Geordie Donna Air found herself interviewing Irish family band The Corrs. Not exactly known for her insightful questioning, Ms Air had viewers choking on their Cheerios when she asked one of the sisters, 'How did you meet?'

✦ ✦ ✦

'I think that the film Clueless *was very deep.*
I think it was deep in the way that it was very light.
I think lightness has to come from a very deep
place if it's true lightness.'

ALICIA SILVERSTONE

Drop Down a Gear

When Jeremy Clarkson, host of the legendary BBC motor programme *Top Gear*, was introduced to supermodel Kate Moss at a party he was understandably keen to impress. Hoping she had a soft spot for wheels he told her, 'I do *Top Gear.*' His comments weren't well received however, and she stormed off. Turns out she thought he was trying to sell her drugs.

✦ ✦ ✦

'I had a huge crush on Olga Korbut, the gymnast. The only other person was Cliff Richard, which is embarrassing – it means that when I was seven I had bad taste and was presumably gay.'

HUGH GRANT

The Miller's Tale

Shortly after watching the film *The Usual Suspects*, Sienna Miller spotted Kevin Spacey in a bar. Excited to find herself so close to one of the film's stars, she approached him and sat down. 'I just wanted to say,' she announced, 'I can't believe I'm sitting in a bar drinking champagne next to Kevin Bacon.' 'Spacey,' Kevin politely corrected. 'Yeah,' Miller replied, 'it is, isn't it?!'

✦ ✦ ✦

'First, let me make it very clear, poor people aren't necessarily killers. Just because you happen to be not rich doesn't mean you're willing to kill.'

GEORGE W. BUSH

Billy's Boat

When Billy Bob Thornton was nominated for the Best
Actor Oscar for his role in *Sling Blade* he declared that
'Getting the nomination is like gravy.' When asked how
he'd feel about winning the award he replied, 'Winning
. . . would be like whatever is better than gravy.' Err,
custard, perhaps?

✦ ✦ ✦

Wiggy Workout

As revenge for what's becoming known
as Lip-Sync-gate, when Elton John publicly
criticized Madonna for not singing live at an awards
ceremony in London, Madge sent Elton some chocolates,
along with a note that read: 'Obviously, [you] just have
too much time on your hands. I figure if you eat all of
these you can spend the next six months in the gym
trying to work them off. Of course, the easiest way for
you to lose ten pounds is to just take off your wig.
Love, Madge.'

Breaking (More Than) the Ice

Charlie's Angels star Lucy Liu has not always been lucky in love. In fact, she's had to break down walls to get men to notice her – literally. 'One time,' she recalled, 'I was trying to get this guy's attention by knocking on a huge window, because I knew he was inside the house somewhere. So I knocked and knocked – and suddenly the window just shattered into a million tiny pieces. That was a special moment.'

✦ ✦ ✦

'Those who survived the San Francisco earthquake said, "Thank God, I'm still alive." But, of course, those who died, their lives will never be the same again.'

SENATOR BARBARA BOXER

*'We're definitely going to get Brooklyn christened,
but we don't know into which religion.'*

DAVID BECKHAM

✦ ✦ ✦

Stage Presence

On stage she's a booty-shaking sexpot, but in interviews
Beyoncé Knowles becomes a God-loving goody-goody.
So disparate are her images that Beyoncé insists the
person up there on stage is not actually her. 'I become a
complete diva. I have a funny voice that I put on,' she
explains. 'It's not me, she's called Sasha.'

✦ ✦ ✦

*'I am intelligent, but I let myself down because
I can't speak properly or spell.'*

JADE GOODY

Cool Britannia

Beyoncé's not the only one suffering from a case of mistaken identity. Britney Spears is another pop star with a split personality. Brit says, 'This alter ego takes over when I am on stage. She is really wild and daring and much more of an impulsive performer than I am.' Her name? 'It's Britannia.' Glad we've cleared that one up.

✦ ✦ ✦

'You don't need to hire a dog therapist, you just need to wake up at 7 a.m. and open the fucking door!'

OZZY OSBOURNE, when wife Sharon told him she'd found a way to stop the dogs pooping on the floor

Wheelie Good Idea

During an interview for Westlife's single 'World Of Our Own', singer Shane Filan revealed that their manager Louis Walsh would stop at nothing to get his band publicity and press coverage. 'He once made me sit in a wheelchair and pretend that I'd been in a fight!' he laughed.

✦ ✦ ✦

Super Sponge

Vegetarian Paul McCartney insisted all the publicity shots for his Super Bowl half-time performance were leather-free. Instead of holding a real football, the superstar held a foam one.

'When I get lonely, I want to be alone. I like to indulge in my loneliness so I can figure out that I'm not really lonely.'

ALICIA SILVERSTONE

✦ ✦ ✦

Spaced Out

Lee Ryan from Blue decided there was only one explanation as to how David Blaine survived during his glass-box stunt (when he was suspended over the banks of the River Thames, near London Bridge, for forty-four days) in 2003. 'I think he's an alien,' he said.

✦ ✦ ✦

'My wife's married. I'm not.'

Basketball star CHARLES BARKLEY to a female photographer

'The idea that marriage has to be for all time –
that I don't understand.'

✦ ✦ ✦

Ring of Truth

In London to record 'Do They Know It's Christmas?' as part of Band Aid 20, teenage star Joss Stone was asked how she felt to be working alongside the legendary Bob Geldof. She looked at the interviewer blank-faced and asked why they were talking about Gandalf from *Lord of the Rings*.

✦ ✦ ✦

'Kurt Russell was sent to us by God. He drew a
circle around us . . . and its powerful alchemy has
protected us ever since.'

Oh, What a Night

A guest on ex-morning show *TV-am* in 1988, comedian
Harry Enfield had the studio in stitches with an
impersonation from his TV show the previous night. Cut
to a giggly Ulrika Jonsson who was due on camera to
present the weather – but unable to get her words out.
When asked what she thought of Harry's impression she
blurted out, 'He was just as good as he was last night!'
. . . before realizing what she was suggesting and giggling
even more.

✦ ✦ ✦

A Step Too Far

Always one for the grand gesture, at the beginning of
U2's 'October' tour Bono marched out into the audience
waving a white flag. On one occasion, however, he
stepped off a balcony . . . into thin air.
Luckily his roadie caught him by
the belt and just about managed to
pull the wriggling rock star back up
onto the balcony. After that, Bono
stopped the flag routine.

Grease *Isn't* the Word

Kate Bosworth isn't too proud to admit she's not the brightest light in Hollywood. The *Blue Crush* beauty said she thought she was signing up for a *Grease* remake when Kevin Spacey approached her for the Bobby Darin biopic *Beyond The Sea*. 'He told me, "I'm doing this movie about Bobby Darin and Sandra Dee,"' the actress recalled. 'I was like, "Sandra Dee from *Grease*? You're making a remake of *Grease*?" He said, "Err, no," and then talked me into doing the film.'

✦ ✦ ✦

Westlife's Willies

Watching Westlife's video for 'If I Let You Go' will never be the same again after the lads let slip a little secret during an interview on music show *The Box*. Shane and co. revealed that as they walk moodily away in the end shot, they all have their bits hanging out. Nice.

It's Raining . . . Pants

Football fan Robbie Williams once threw £2,000 out of a bedroom window simply because his favourite team, Port Vale Football Club, were playing a match that day. His mum Jan was not too happy, however. Not because he'd wasted money, but because he got so carried away with the moment that he'd grabbed her bras and knickers and chucked them out too.

✦ ✦ ✦

'I gave Paris Hilton a rat called Tori Spelling for Christmas, and Paris loved her. Rats make great pets. I told Tori about how I named my rat after her, and Tori said that it was funny, but I could tell it hurt her feelings. Tori felt that I think her face looks like a rat's, but I actually own six rats and I named each after a character on Beverly Hills 90210, *like Shannen Doherty and Luke Perry. But Tori didn't know that, so she was upset.'*

NICOLE RICHIE

'I wouldn't run for US president. I wouldn't want to move to a smaller house.'

BONO

✦ ✦ ✦

Hot Head

Britney Spears had a lucky escape after her hair caught fire when she leaned over a candle during a visit to a Hollywood spa. Thankfully her masseuse was on hand to extinguish the flames with a bucket of water.

✦ ✦ ✦

'I look at every person on this planet and realize that they were all a baby at one point.'

DREW BARRYMORE

+ + +

Hot House

In March 2002, Britney Spears had a second fire-related accident when she almost burned down her New York apartment. 'Brit had left a candle burning in front of an air vent [and gone shopping],' her mother, Lynne, recalled. 'The wall caught on fire, and the fire department had to come to put it out.'

+ + +

'To say this book is about me is ridiculous. This book is not about me.'

Model KATE MOSS on her book,
Kate: The Kate Moss Book

✦ ✦ ✦

Telling Times

As rumours of feuds within the Labour government continued to be reported in the press, a key member of Blair's cabinet made a telling slip of the tongue on national TV. During a televised debate in March 2004, Labour MP Harriet Harman referred to Chancellor Gordon Brown as 'Prime Minister'. Bet there was a slap on the wrist for her later.

✦ ✦ ✦

'Let me tell you something: you have not partied till you've partied at dawn in complete silence with Buddhist monks.'

CAMERON DIAZ

Funny Girl

Canadian pop star Avril Lavigne takes April Fools' Day jokes to the extreme. Examples include telling her mother she was pregnant, and calling her manager and telling him she'd been in a terrible accident and was in hospital with head injuries. Unless of course the first story was true and her mum had just reacted badly to the baby news . . .

✦ ✦ ✦

'When I'm working well I like to think I'm doing God's work.'

FAYE DUNAWAY

✦ ✦ ✦

Bald Boy

Friends star Matt LeBlanc was spotted stocking up on Rogaine, the men's hair restorer, at a Malibu supermarket in 2004. When a sheepish-looking Matt was asked by an inquisitive shopper, 'Are you losing yours then?' the actor shot back, 'It's for my friend, seriously – you see he's too embarrassed to go buy it himself.'

✦ ✦ ✦

Lord of the Lizard

Perhaps confirming some people's suspicions about
drama-school syllabuses, Orlando Bloom studied animals
to improve his acting technique. However, it was the
lizards he loved best, who captivated him with their
stillness and composure. 'We had to go to the zoo, watch
the animals, then mimic their behaviour. I studied them
and all but ended up being a lizard.' Err, come again?

✦ ✦ ✦

> *'Men, I want you just thinking of one word all season. One word and one word only: Super Bowl.'*

BILL PETERSEN

✦ ✦ ✦

Dog-tired

As perhaps befitting a multi-millionaire heiress, Paris Hilton's infamous carefree style had studio bosses panicking when she arrived late for her part of a TV-presenting job in April 2005. While other celebs had no problem turning up on time, Hilton's arrival over an hour late was the cause of much consternation. Her response when host Ryan Seacrest enquired as to her tardiness? 'I was walking my dog.'

✦ ✦ ✦

> *'Strangely, in the slow-motion replay, the ball seemed to hang in the air for even longer.'*

DAVID ACFIELD

Towel Tester

Angelina Jolie stunned shop assistants at Macy's store in Los Angeles when she took a selection of towels into the changing rooms to try them out. She told shop staff she needed to rub them against her body to check whether they were soft enough. Like you do.

✦ ✦ ✦

Gere's Tears

One day in 1995, on the set of *First Knight*, Richard Gere arrived late for filming, much to co-star Sean Connery's annoyance. The Scottish actor reportedly growled at Gere, 'Where have you been? You want to get a move on.' When the scene was complete Gere, clearly upset, retired to his trailer, and later sent an assistant with a message telling Connery of his distress. 'A fuss about nothing,' Connery retorted – 'You get this on film sets.'

+ + +

Manson's Mane

Dita Von Teese, the fiancée of goth-rocker Marilyn
Manson, somewhat punctured her man's rock
credentials when she revealed during an
interview that Manson had a thing for hair-
straightening irons. Dita complained
she could never find the
straighteners because her
scary- looking boyfriend was
always using them. She said, 'It's not very rock, but how
else could he achieve his sexy, straight look?'

+ + +

✦ ✦ ✦

Russell's Writing

Following the birth of his son Charles in 2003, hardman Russell Crowe suddenly revealed his softer side. Russ penned a heartfelt open letter to mark the boy's first birthday – even though Charles couldn't read yet. He wrote: 'Dear Charlie, our beautiful boy. You were born a year ago and it has been the most wonderful year. You are a very special little boy – so affectionate and lovely. I'm going to wake you up in a minute and give you your First Birthday Bottle.'

✦ ✦ ✦

'I bought all those Jane Fonda exercise videos. I love to sit and eat cookies and watch them.'

DOLLY PARTON

Thanks for the Mammories

The World Wide Web never had so many hits as when people clambered to watch the performance of Janet Jackson and Justin Timberlake at the 2004 Super Bowl Concert in America. Janet set off a furore when she bared her breast during a half-time song-and-dance routine with Mr Timberlake. At the end of a song titled 'Rock Your Body', Jackson allowed Timberlake to rip away the leather cup covering her breast, as they sang: 'Gonna have you naked by the end of this song' – exposing a bosom to some 100 million viewers. The moment was made even more memorable, and shocking to some, because Jackson's breast was adorned with a sun-shaped metal ring that pierced the nipple. When middle America reacted in outrage, 'offended' by the sight of Janet's jug, the Jackson/Timberlake camp denied it was part of the act. A new term, 'wardrobe malfunction', was born.

✦ ✦ ✦

*'The only reason I ever started singing is because
I wanted to own a Krispy Kreme doughnut shop.'*

USHER

'I've learned when I see a flag in a relationship the next time, recognize it as a flag. Don't think, "Oh that's just a shadow." That's a flag.'

HALLE BERRY

✦ ✦ ✦

Smelly Spears

One day in December 2004, Britney Spears doffed her shoes during a flight from LA to New York. The result? 'The smell was unbelievable,' another passenger later reported. 'One woman had a word with the air hostess, then three or four others complained. She looked pretty embarrassed as she tapped Britney on the shoulder and asked her very politely to put her shoes back on. Britney went red, laughed and said her shoes make her feet stink. Thankfully she put them back on.'

✦ ✦ ✦

'Man, I know what DNA stands for – Dis Negro is Attractive. Aiiiight!'

Big Brother 5's VICTOR EBUWA

This award goes to . . . not you!

Confusing a birthday cake with an Artist of the Millennium award, Michael Jackson was left red-faced when he mistakenly 'accepted' the non-existent award from Britney Spears, live, in front of millions of viewers, at the 2002 MTV Video Music Awards. As she summoned him to the stage in order to present to him with a cake for his forty-fourth birthday, he misunderstood her when she announced that, for her, Jackson was the artist of the millennium. His emotional acceptance speech included thanking God, his parents, and the illusionist David Blaine. 'When I was a little boy growing up in Indiana, if someone told me I'd be getting the Artist of the Millennium award, I'd never have believed it,' he said. MTV claimed afterwards it was all 'a bit of a misunderstanding'.

✦ ✦ ✦

'If you're sitting around after a show and there's something on [TV] you don't like, you just switch it off by throwing a bottle through the screen.'

KEITH RICHARDS

Judy's Jugs

On stage at the National TV Awards in 2000 with her husband Richard Madeley to collect the best daytime programme award for *This Morning*, Judy Finnegan gave viewers a treat they weren't expecting. As the pair thanked the voters, Judy's black dress gradually fell open, exposing a (shock!) dodgy white bra underneath. It was only when fellow presenter John Leslie rushed to the stage to cover her modesty that either she or Richard noticed what had happened. Her husband quipped: 'If you vote for us next year she will show you both of them.'

✦ ✦ ✦

I'm Not your Man?

EastEnders actor Shane Richie was left red-faced when a radio station refused to play his former number-one single, 'I'm Your Man' – despite him phoning in to request it personally. 'It wasn't on our playlist so we offered to play the Wham version,' laughed Heart FM DJ Paul Bryant.

Fern's Fancies

Bubbly TV host Fern Britton collapsed in giggles on *This Morning* while apologizing to a shocked neighbour for a full-frontal flash. Fern and co-presenter Phillip Schofield wept tears of laughter as Fern described the moment she was spied stark naked. Fern, tongue-in-cheek, said: 'Something very embarrassing happened to me yesterday. I had been in the garden all day and my daughter and I'd been planting up pots of earth and plants. When it was bath time for my daughter, because she's only two, I said, "You know, I'm going to get in the bath with you." So I was completely naked and then I thought, "While I'm doing this I'll just close this sash window," bearing in mind this is 5 p.m. So I got to the window and it's a little bit sticky and I'm pushing up against the glass.' She gasped: 'We have a shared drive and our neighbour drove in, saw me and waved at me!'

✦ ✦ ✦

'I've never done it and I never will. It would freak me out. If anyone even touches my arsehole, I'll kick them in the nuts.'

KELLY OSBOURNE – on anal sex

Meryl's Mishap

Accepting an award on behalf of screenwriter Charlie
Kaufman at the 2003 BAFTA film awards, Meryl Streep
made an unintentional gaffe. While reading from
Kaufman's thank-you speech she said, 'I'd like to spank
Spike Jonze' – cut to ripples of laughter from the celeb-
packed audience.

✦ ✦ ✦

MICHELLE: *What are you thinking about?*

STUART: *Nothing, what are you thinking about?*

MICHELLE: *I was thinking, 'What's Stuart thinking
about?'*

**The romance between *Big Brother 5*'s
MICHELLE BASS and STUART WILSON
took a while to get off the ground**

*'Liam's like a woman on a fucking permanent
menstrual cycle about everything. He's either way
up in the clouds or way down in the gutter.'*

NOEL GALLAGHER

✦ ✦ ✦

Fabio-lous

In 1999, Italian male supermodel Fabio was one of the
first people to enjoy the thrills of the 'Apollo's Chariot'
rollercoaster at Busch Gardens in Virginia. While he had
a great time, one particular incident no doubt marred the
experience for him: a 20-pound goose caught him square
in the face and gave him a bloody nose.

✦ ✦ ✦

*'I could get into bed with James Bond, then take
my false leg off and it would really be a gun.'*

HEATHER MILLS

'We're all here for the same reason: to love me.'

BARRY MANILOW to his fans in New York

✦ ✦ ✦

Kiss Diss

It won't do much for Jennifer Lopez's confidence to hear that hunky French actor Michael Vartan was less than enthralled by her tongue technique in their *Monster-In-Law* kissing scenes. *Alias* star Vartan, who was also the handsome teacher Drew Barrymore fell for in *Never Been Kissed*, said, 'There was nothing romantic about it.' So what was he thinking when he locked lips with J-Lo? 'You'd be surprised,' he said. 'Like, literally, "What time is lunch?"'

✦ ✦ ✦

'I know the human being and fish can coexist peacefully.'

GEORGE W. BUSH

Just Ribbing

Of the many rumours circulating about him, Manson himself addressed the most notorious one of all. 'People say that I removed my two bottom ribs so that I could perform oral sex on myself, but that's untrue,' he explained. 'The operation was far too expensive.'

✦ ✦ ✦

Off with your . . . erm, Cock

Goth rocker Marilyn Manson was once asked what was the oddest thing that had happened to him on tour. 'I was arrested in Rome,' he replied. 'Not for wearing a pope's outfit – which I think was the reason they wanted to arrest me, but it wasn't illegal – but someone came with a complaint from a concert that happened two years prior, saying that I pulled off my genitals and threw them to the audience.' He paused before adding, 'At that show, I did not throw my genitals. I still have them.'

Bedroom Story

Writer Mark Twain wrote most of his books in bed, propped up on pillows. He loved his home comforts so much in fact that he even insisted on being interviewed from between the sheets. When his wife suggested this might be seen as a bit odd, he offered to have another bed made up for the reporter.

✦ ✦ ✦

'These, they're very dangerous. They trap you. Especially these furry ones . . . it's these furry guys that get you in real trouble. They can reach out and listen to something so – keep it respectful here.'

GEORGE W. BUSH'S advice to Arnold Schwarzenegger
about being careful when speaking near microphones

REPORTER: *Did you realize you have five gold albums in Germany and Austria?*

DAVID HASSELHOFF: *Where's Austria?*

＋ ＋ ＋

Hair-raising Stuff

Matthew McConaughey and Penelope Cruz became real-life lovers after starring together in action movie *Sahara*. When making the film, Cruz happily made do with the production's hair stylist and make-up guy. McConaughey, on the other hand, insisted that he needed his own personal make-up artist and hair stylist and two hair colourists.

＋ ＋ ＋

'The senator has got to understand if he's going to have – he can't have it both ways. He can't take the high horse and then claim the low road!'

GEORGE W. BUSH

'Rio de Janeiro, ain't that a person?'

JADE GOODY

✦ ✦ ✦

Balls to the Lot of You

In 1988, during a press call for the world's media, former President George Bush Snr attempted to get 'down' with the voters by proving he was a fun-loving guy. The venue? A ten-pin bowling alley. The outcome? He fell arse over tit before he could even let go of the ball.

✦ ✦ ✦

'I put on fifteen pounds recently, just for fun.'

DARYL HANNAH

*'I would like to live for ever, because we should
not live for ever, because if we were ever supposed
to live for ever, then we would live for ever, but we
cannot live for ever, which is why I would not live
for ever.'*

MISS ALABAMA, in the 1994 Miss Universe contest

✦ ✦ ✦

Maggie's Mind Scramble

During a live phone-in on BBC's *Election Call* in 1983,
Maggie Thatcher let down her iron guard and appeared a
little confused. As host Robin Day took a call from a
viewer called Mr Crawford, Mags didn't seem to know
where the voice on the end of the phone was coming
from. 'Can *you* see Mr Crawford?' she asked Robin Day.
'No,' came the bemused reply. 'He's on the *phone.*'

✦ ✦ ✦

'It's Mona Lisa *who's symmetrical, innit?'*

JADE . . . again

Take a Bite

It was one of the oddest announcements of the year. When Gwyneth Paltrow and Coldplay frontman Chris Martin had their first daughter they decided to name her after a piece of fruit. When interviewed on *The Tonight With Jay Leno* show in America, Gwyneth admitted she'd taken the name 'Apple' to global extremes. 'I've started calling her Apple in different languages,' she said, 'like "Yabushko" is Polish, or "Pomme" in France. Or "Mansana" in Japanese.' Leno replied, 'This kid is gonna need therapy by the time it's four years old!' Then he concluded, 'It is a sweet name . . . unless you're a little fat girl . . . and you don't want to go with Pear!'

✦ ✦ ✦

'More and more of our imports are coming from overseas.'

GEORGE W. BUSH

Achtung Harry

While his brother William has kept his head down and his reputation intact, Prince Harry is rarely out of hot water (or the papers) as a young adult. One particularly memorable gaffe was the outfit he chose to wear to a fancy-dress party. The prince was pictured in the *Sun* newspaper wearing a Nazi uniform complete with swastika armband. Amid general indignation (insulting British Jews; gross lapse of taste; young man unfit for the Army, and so on), he was asked to apologize to the nation at large. Fortunately for him, Clarence House concluded he'd already done enough and ruled against allowing him to speak.

✦ ✦ ✦

'I'm not a snob. Ask anybody. Well, anybody who matters.'

SIMON LE BON

> *'I'd like to play passionate women, but*
> *no one will let me.'*

RUSSELL CROWE

+ + +

Down Blunder

The Duke of Edinburgh is notorious for his insensitive slip-ups. On a tour of Commonwealth countries with the Queen as part of her Jubilee year celebrations in 2002, he was introduced to William Brim, the aboriginal owner of a cultural park in Cairns, Queensland. Phil then proceeded to ask him: 'Do you still throw spears at each other?'
Mr Brim replied: 'No, sir. We don't throw spears any more.'

+ + +

> *'I swear to God, you can be in the shittiest mood*
> *and brush your teeth, and suddenly you feel like a*
> *champion.'*

SHIA LABEOUF

Pain and Pretzels

In January 2002, Dubya reached such a fever pitch of
excitement while watching an NFL play-off game that he
choked on a pretzel and fainted. As a result of the savoury-
induced swoon, the President of the United States banged
his head, but recovered a few seconds later. A top aide
reported that Bush had said that, following the incident,
'his dogs were looking at him funny'. Hmm . . .

✦ ✦ ✦

Mad For It

On 18 October 2000, future president George W. Bush –
noted for his tendency to stumble over polysyllabic words
– delivered a speech in St Louis, Missouri. 'If affirmative
action means what I just described, what I'm for,' he
declared, 'then I'm for it.'

'I think Renée [Zellweger] is incredible. She's like pizza, you know, in that she's always good.'

CHARLIZE THERON

✦ ✦ ✦

Pissing About

During a royal visit to an Australian cotton farm in 2000, the Duke of Edinburgh was handed a piezometer, a device commonly used to measure the depth of water in soil, after which he replied to a startled farmer, 'Surely you mean a pissometer?'

✦ ✦ ✦

'There is no doubt in my mind that this country cannot achieve any objective we put our mind to.'

GEORGE W. BUSH

'Richard doesn't really like me to kill bugs, but sometimes I can't help it.'

CINDY CRAWFORD about her ex, Richard Gere

✦ ✦ ✦

Bloody Hell!

When Angelina Jolie met British actor Jonny Lee Miller on the set of the film *Hackers* they fell in love and briefly married. For their wedding ceremony, Jolie chose not to wear the traditional white dress . . . and turned up instead wearing rubber trousers and a white shirt on which Miller's name was written in blood.

✦ ✦ ✦

'I am not a demon. I am a lizard, a shark, a heat-seeking panther.'

NICOLAS CAGE

Odd Bods

Jolie's second husband was the actor Billy Bob Thornton, and the public displays of affection were no less peculiar. They allegedly bonded over a bridge where both had considered suicide, waltzed about with one another's blood in vials around their necks, purchased his'n'hers grave plots and talked openly of their padded sex room. They were married for just three years.

✦ ✦ ✦

Nappy Chappy

Following a performance at a venue in the north of England, Marilyn Manson decided to leave a special present behind in his dressing room for the cleaners. So what did he leave? Chocolates? Flowers? A signed photograph? Well, no. Manson left quite a different momento – a nappy full of poo (and let's just say, there were no kids on tour with him).

Room With a (Not Very Pleasant) View

Kevin 'Six Degrees' Bacon received more hospitality perks than he bargained for while staying in London during a filming stint – a collection of sex toys was stored in the room's cupboard. He said, 'They had a thing called a smut drawer and I opened it up and it was filled with sex toys and you could just take them out. There were things that required batteries. It was amazing. They had something that I'd never seen before called Banana Dick Lick Oil . . . and then they had wrist restraints and as I climbed into bed that night I thought, "I'm not really sure I want to be in these sheets right now."'

✦ ✦ ✦

'I have talismans that remind me of things that I may be forgetting during the day – whether it's to be present or to breathe.'

ALANIS MORISSETTE

'I'm getting more famouser by the day.'

AVRIL LAVIGNE

+ + +

'I've got ten pairs of trainers. That's one for every day of the week.'

SAM FOX

+ + +

'What I'd really like to do is dissolve religious conflict.'

PINK

'I like a girl to whom you can say at 2 a.m., "Let's go jet-skiing!" – who doesn't mind getting wet.'

ENRIQUE IGLESIAS

✦ ✦ ✦

Batty Boy

Following the vial of her blood that Billy Bob Thornton carried around his neck, Angelina Jolie reportedly gave new beau Brad Pitt a vial of grey powder with the power to dispel accidents. Turns out that the grey powder was the burned remains of a bat. Well, that's OK then.

✦ ✦ ✦

'I would not wish to be Prime Minister, dear.'

MARGARET THATCHER in 1973

Swanks a Lot

In 2000, Hilary Swank won an Academy Award for her portrayal of Brandon Teena in *Boys Don't Cry*. Not expecting to win, Hils hadn't prepared a formal speech, but once on stage she managed to remember everyone she wished to thank, with one minor exception. Her husband.

✦ ✦ ✦

It's a Steal

In April 2003, the *San Francisco Examiner* reported 'Goldie Hawn isn't Hollywood's most observant star.' The reason? The actress's Porsche was stolen from right in front of her house, but she didn't realize it was gone until three days later.

'I always felt like my twenties were like waiting to board an aeroplane. I was in the departure lounge of who I really am.'

GERI HALLIWELL

+ + +

Burnt Sausage

Perhaps not demonstrating the greatest example ever of responsible kitchen craft, the Naked Chef lived up to his name when, on Valentine's Day 2004, Jamie Oliver rustled a little something up as a surprise for his wife, Jools – while completely naked. Unfortunately, in doing so, he burnt his penis on the oven door. 'It really ruined my evening,' he recalled, 'and my night.'

+ + +

'I get to go to lots of overseas places, like Canada.'

BRITNEY SPEARS, from the USA

> *'My sister's expecting a baby, and I don't know if I'm going to be an uncle or an aunt.'*
>
> CHUCK NEVITT, basketball player

✦ ✦ ✦

In the Buff

While filming *Buffy the Vampire Slayer*, Sarah Michelle Gellar drove to the studio early one morning. 'I'd worked all night,' she later recalled, 'and was at cracking point.' While driving, Gellar noticed that she was subject to more-than-customary attention. The problem? 'I looked down – and realized I'd never put my dress on!'

✦ ✦ ✦

> *'This is Gregoriava from Bulgaria. I saw her snatch this morning and it was amazing.'*
>
> PAT GLENN, weightlifting commentator

'The bowler's Holding, the batsman's Willey.'

BRIAN JOHNSTON

+ + +

'I'm just glad it'll be Clark Gable who's falling on his face and not Gary Cooper.'

GARY COOPER, on his decision not to take
the leading role in *Gone With the Wind*

+ + +

'I have always found strangers sexy.'

HUGH GRANT, six months before being
arrested with Divine Brown

Red-faced Ryan

Meg Ryan was left red-faced after her credit card was rejected in top American store Bloomingdale's. The star racked up $1,000 on baby clothes (a gift for a friend's little one, apparently), but ditsy Ryan offered an American Express card that had expired. 'She was furious at first, but when she realized her mistake she was very apologetic,' revealed the shop assistant. 'She explained she'd forgotten to cut the old one up.'

✦ ✦ ✦

Lost or Stolen?

Paris Hilton's extra-curricular activities found their way into the public domain when in 2005 some scally got hold of her mobile phone and consequently all its contents found their way onto the World Wide Web. Gems included over 500 celebrities' phone numbers (including those of Sienna Miller and Black Eyed Peas singer Fergie, (who said, 'I'm going to kill Paris Hilton'). Also available for viewing were pics of a topless Ms Hilton snogging a female pal, and reminders to get such things as the 'birth-control pill'.

Nurse Forgetty

Actress Renée Zellweger had Hugh Grant to thank for 'stalling' for her during the Golden Globe Awards in 2001, at which she was declared Best Actress for her eponymous lead role in *Nurse Betty*. The audience were kept waiting as Zellweger returned from the toilet; Grant joked that she was hiding under a table. 'I had lipstick on my teeth,' she explained to the celebrities gathered in Los Angeles.

◆ ◆ ◆

'I believe that, as quickly as possible, young cows ought to be allowed to go across our border.'

GEORGE W. BUSH, in Ottawa, Canada

'Now is not the time for sound bites. I can feel the hand of history on my shoulder.'

TONY BLAIR

+ + +

Lost Lyrics

Rock gods are humans too, and Bono is certainly no exception. Being particularly absent-minded, however, can be a bit of a setback, when, for example, you lose all the lyrics to your new album (*October*) shortly before going into the studio to record it. Doh!

+ + +

'I cannot tell you how grateful I am – I am filled with humidity.'

GIB LEWIS, Texas House Speaker

'Fiction writing is great, you can make up almost anything.'

IVANA TRUMP, on finishing her first novel

✦ ✦ ✦

Drawer? What Drawer?

In Billy Wilder's *Some Like It Hot*, a particular scene required Marilyn Monroe to request a drink from a bottle placed in a dresser drawer. As straightforward as this sounds, Monroe just couldn't get the line right. 'On the fifty-third take,' Wilder later recalled, 'I told her we had put the line on pieces of paper and they were in every drawer she would open . . . She went to the wrong piece of furniture.'

✦ ✦ ✦

'You guys line up alphabetically by height.'

BILL PETERSEN, Florida State football coach

Lucky Old Dog

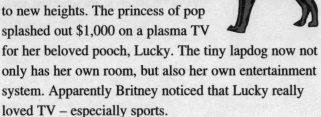

Britney Spears has taken puppy love
to new heights. The princess of pop
splashed out $1,000 on a plasma TV
for her beloved pooch, Lucky. The tiny lapdog now not
only has her own room, but also her own entertainment
system. Apparently Britney noticed that Lucky really
loved TV – especially sports.

✦ ✦ ✦

I'll Have a Bit(bit) of that, Please

Britney caused controversy again after ordering a £100
steak at a swish hotel – then feeding it to another of her
pet pooches. The singer bought the pricey meal for her
spoilt chihuahua, Bitbit, at the award-winning Picasso
Hotel in Las Vegas, infuriating head chef Julian Serrano
in the process.

✦ ✦ ✦

*'It's clearly a budget. It's got a lot of numbers
in it.'*

GEORGE W. BUSH

✦ ✦ ✦

Waterlogged

You hear complaints about London tap water, but few
have taken such extreme lengths to avoid it than
supermodel Kate Moss, who at one time had 40 litres of
mineral water a day delivered to her house. Given that
she was reputed to have bathed in champagne with ex-
boyf Johnny Depp, rumours were that she was bathing in
the mineral water to look after her valuable skin.

✦ ✦ ✦

Carey's closet

Most people have a drawer set aside for underwear –
loaded Mariah Carey has an entire wardrobe. And, of
course, such an extensive collection needs a foolproof
system of categorization.'OK, I also have a robe, some
slippers and a pair of boxer shorts in there, but ignore
that. I like lingerie that's lacy and normally white. But
then I also love dressing up in pink lingerie – and black is
hot too. I have everything laid out in colours so I can pick
them out quickly. It's right off my bathroom so rather
than going down to my main closet soaking wet, all
dripping and nude, I decided to make a nice lingerie
closet. That way I can jump out of my tub, run naked into
the next room and put on a nice little number.'

✦ ✦ ✦

'I'd kill myself if I was as fat as Marilyn Monroe.'

ELIZABETH HURLEY

'If my jeans could talk, would I be embarrassed?'

BROOKE SHIELDS

✦ ✦ ✦

Stone the Crows!

In London, while filming the sequel to *Basic Instinct*, Sharon Stone and a female pal went for dinner at posh restaurant The Wolseley. At least you'd think'd have gone out for dinner. As soon as Sharon sat down, she whipped out a chessboard from her bag and set it up on the table. 'They looked deadly serious about the game,' said a fellow diner. 'The waiters had trouble fitting the food on the table so they had to balance the plates around the board.' At least when she paid the bill they could ask her for the cheque (mate) . . .

✦ ✦ ✦

'I have opinions of my own – strong opinions – but I don't always agree with them.'

GEORGE W. BUSH

Pet Passengers

After a visit to Las Vegas in February 2004, Paris Hilton arrived at the airport for a flight home to Los Angeles and attempted to board the plane with some recent purchases – including a goat. 'The flight attendants thought I was insane,' she recalled. 'They were like, "This isn't a travelling circus."' Paris, who was also travelling with a monkey and a ferret, decided instead to treat her new pets to a six-hour limousine ride home.

✦ ✦ ✦

'If only faces could talk . . . '

PAT SUMMERALL, commentator during the Super Bowl

✦ ✦ ✦

Pants to That

Whenever Renée Zellweger goes abroad, her underwear travels separately so that customs don't get to snoop at them. 'I can't bear the idea of them checking out my smalls in front of me,' she admits, 'so I send those to my home by FedEx and collect all those boxes of used knickers when I get back.' Nice.

*'There aren't many big words I don't know,
but I hate people who use big words.'*

PATRICK SWAYZE

✦ ✦ ✦

Barking Mad

In the early days of her marriage to Chris Martin,
Gwyneth Paltrow discovered a strange new relaxation
technique that involved her barking like a dog each
morning. The actress, a huge fan of alternative therapies,
said she was introduced to the bizarre practice by her pal
Sting, who told her it helped people to get in touch with
their 'inner voice'.

✦ ✦ ✦

'Solutions are not the answer.'

RICHARD NIXON

Michael O'Mara Humour

All Michael O'Mara titles are available by post from:
Bookpost, PO Box 29, Douglas, Isle of Man, IM99 1BQ

Credit cards accepted. Telephone: 01624 677237 Fax: 01624 670923
Email: bookshop@enterprise.net Internet: www.bookpost.co.uk

Free postage and packing in the UK.

Other Michael O'Mara Humour titles:

The Book of Urban Legends	ISBN 1-85479-932-0 pb £3.99
Born for the Job	ISBN 1-84317-099-X pb £5.99
The Complete Book of Farting	ISBN 1-85479-440-X pb £4.99
The Ultimate Insult	ISBN 1-85479-288-1 pb £5.99
Wicked Cockney Rhyming Slang	ISBN 1-85479-386-1 pb £3.99
The Wicked Wit of Jane Austen	ISBN 1-85479-652-6 hb £9.99
The Wicked Wit of Winston Churchill	ISBN 1-85479-529-5 hb £9.99
The Wicked Wit of Oscar Wilde	ISBN 1-85479-542-2 hb £9.99
The World's Stupidest Laws	ISBN 1-85479-549-X pb £3.99
The World's Stupidest Signs	ISBN 1-85479-555-4 pb £3.99
More of the World's Stupidest Signs	ISBN 1-84317-032-9 pb £4.99
The World's Stupidest Last Words	ISBN 1-84317-021-3 pb £4.99
The World's Stupidest Inventions	ISBN 1-84317-036-1 pb £5.99
The World's Stupidest Instructions	ISBN 1-84317-078-7 pb £4.99
The World's Stupidest Sporting Screw-Ups	ISBN 1-84317-039-6 pb £4.99
The World's Stupidest Chat-Up Lines	ISBN 1-84317-019-1 pb £4.99
The World's Stupidest Headlines	ISBN 1-84317-105-8 pb £4.99
The World's Stupidest Deaths	ISBN 1-84317-136-8 pb £4.99
Cricket: It's A Funny Old Game	ISBN 1-84317-090-6 pb £4.99
Football: It's A Funny Old Game	ISBN 1-84317-091-4 pb £4.99
Laughable Latin	ISBN 1-84317-097-3 pb £4.99
School Rules	ISBN 1-84317-100-7 pb £4.99
Sex Cheques (new edition)	ISBN 1-84317-121-X pb £3.50
The Timewaster Letters	ISBN 1-84317-108-2 pb £9.99
The Jordan Joke Book	ISBN 1-84317-120-1 pb £4.99
Speak Well English	ISBN 1-84317-088-4 pb £5.99
Shite's Unoriginal Miscellany	ISBN 1-84317-064-7 hb £9.99
Eats, Shites & Leaves	ISBN 1-84317-098-1 hb £9.99
A Shite History of Nearly Everything	ISBN 1-84317-138-4 hb £9.99